. . . . a cord

three strands is

easily broken. Eccl.

April 12, 2008

from
Bob + Sandra Sommer

P9-DTN-858

Also by June Cotner

To Have and To Hold

PRAYERS, POEMS, AND
BLESSINGS FOR *Newlyweds*

June Cotner

CENTER
STREET

NEW YORK   BOSTON   NASHVILLE

Compilation Copyright © 2007 by June Cotner Graves
Foreword Copyright © 2007 by June Cotner Graves
All rights reserved. Except as permitted under the U.S. Copyright Act of 1976,
no part of this publication may be reproduced, distributed, or transmitted in
any form or by any means, or stored in a database or retrieval system,
without the prior written permission of the publisher.

Center Street
Hachette Book Group, USA
237 Park Avenue
New York, NY 10169

Visit our Web site at www.centerstreet.com.

Center Street is a division of Hachette Book Group USA.
The Center Street name and logo are trademarks of Hachette Book Group USA.

Printed in the United States of America

First Edition: April 2007
10 9 8 7 6 5 4 3 2 1

Library of Congress Cataloging-in-Publication Data
ISBN-10: 1-931722-91-9
ISBN-13: 978-1-931722-91-9
LCCN: 2006928809

For my dear, loving husband,

Jim

Thanks

I'm deeply grateful to my husband, Jim, whose continued companionship is so important to me. I see and feel experiences from my early marriage echoed in the words of the poets in this book. I'm thankful to my daughter, Kirsten, whose marriage also served as inspiration for this collection and who offered a newlywed's fresh perspective on these poems. Thanks also to my son, Kyle, for his help and support behind the scenes, and to my dear friends and extended family who enrich my life in many ways.

I'm very thankful to Rolf Zettersten, publisher of Center Street; my attentive editor, Chris Park; and the tireless, committed people at Hachette Book Group USA: Chip MacGregor, associate publisher; Lori Quinn, associate publisher, marketing; Preston Cannon, director, advertising and promotion; Jana Burson, director of publicity; Penina Sacks, production editor; Kelly A. Berry and Sarah Sper, editorial assistants. I greatly value all their support.

As always, huge thanks go to my longtime literary agent, Denise Marcil. I am so fortunate to have her as a friend and guide to accompany me through my professional endeavors. As she has done so many times before, she believed in this book, found the right house, and gave me encouragement throughout the process.

Creating anthologies has brought so many talented poets into my daily life, and *To Have and to Hold* would not have been possible without them. Their unique, eloquent poems deserve my highest recognition and appreciation. Even those poets who didn't make it into this collection have blessed my life with their honest and heartfelt words. I'm grateful for the enthusiasm and understanding of all who submitted to *To Have and to Hold*.

Members of my community have extended themselves in the creation of this book, just as they have with my many others. The staff at the Poulsbo library deserves a special salute, as does Suzanne Droppert, owner of Liberty Bay Books, who is constantly helpful and generous to me. I'm also deeply grateful for my assistant in the office, Ryan Mann, who has lent a hand in editing, reading submissions, obtaining permissions, and producing this book. Above all, I wouldn't have the opportunity to do the work I love without the support of the community of readers who purchase my anthologies. It brings me joy to know that my books have become part of their lives.

Finally, I would like to thank God, whose hand guided me to my husband, blessed me as a newlywed, and continues to bring joy into my life each day.

Contents

3. Toasts

4. Daily Life

5. Romance

6. Intimacy

7. Reflections

8. Inspiration

A Letter to Readers

No matter how long you and your spouse have loved each other, and no matter what you've already experienced together, the transition into married life will change you in the most beautifully unexpected ways. As you build the foundation of your life together, your different habits, varying expectations, and unique ways of communicating will make your marriage a special monument that will last a lifetime. *To Have and to Hold* is a compilation specifically created for newlyweds that will provide comfort and encouragement as you live through some of the most blissful and important years of your life.

I look back fondly on my own experience as a newlywed, when my husband and I were learning to live and love together as a married couple and beginning to face the world's challenges and accept its rewards. In many ways, those early years were starkly beautiful and simple, but they also brought a few hurdles. I remain amazed at how much was possible with love, laughter, tenderness, and understanding.

In the past few years, as I've watched my daughter go through that same process in her new marriage, I connected increasingly to poems about the newlywed experience. I knew I needed to create a book in which writers could share a variety of perspectives, thoughts, and observations with newlyweds who could benefit from them. In order to make *To Have and to Hold* a reality, I drew from many trusted contributors who've submitted work to my collections for years, but I also read many submissions from first-time contributors. Others sent poems and quotations that had inspired, moved, or touched them. After reading and enjoying them all, I narrowed the field by selecting pieces that spoke to the hearts of newlyweds—the excitement, the hope, the dreams. I then shared them with my daughter, ensuring that reading this book would be a life-enriching experience for newlyweds and one that would celebrate the possibilities of those first few years of a lifelong journey.

Countless books offer instructions on how to make marriage a lasting bond. This proves one thing: there's no single way to create a strong marriage. For that reason, I've avoided prescriptive writing and instead selected poems, prayers, and inspirational pieces that are personal in their approach and that reflect the wide range of emotions and experiences of life as newlyweds. The pieces are arranged in sections to aid those in search of a prayer or poem to fit a particular mood or occasion. While some of the selections, especially those in the sections "Prayers," "Blessings," and "Toasts," can be used for reading at a wedding ceremony, most of the pieces in this book are for your life together after the ceremony. The other chapters ("Daily Life," "Romance," "Intimacy," "Reflections," and "Inspiration") will lend insight into how to nourish your new marriage.

I hope that all the poems in *To Have and to Hold* will provide an uplifting and enriching reading experience and that you'll enjoy them with your spouse as a way to celebrate the union of your lives. After reading this book, I hope you'll come away with greater appreciation of your new marriage and gain your own unique insight into how to make it a rewarding lifetime bond.

1

Prayers

A Newlywed's Prayer

Lord, bless us and keep us always with You.
Open our eyes to see each other as You see us.
Open our hearts to love each other as You love us.
Open our minds to the wonder and mystery
of who You are
and of who You have created
each of us to be.
And let us spend our lifetimes together.

—*Sally Clark*

Prayer for Fruit

O God, teach us to be always
freely giving, living in love.
Remind us often to voice praise
to each other and You above.

Let our love be ever joyful,
new, renewed every week and year.
Let us be content and peaceful,
Thrilled to sense You are very near.

May our love with patience expand
as we still wait on You in prayer.
With kindness let us lend a hand,
encouraging some other pair.

Show Your goodness through us, we pray
in words of love and generous acts.
Keep us faithful in every way,
shielded from devious attacks.

Let self-control and gentleness
channel our thoughts and feelings toward
whatever is true, right, and best:
may our union shine for You, Lord.

—*Marjorie Gray*

The Dark Side of Love

Lord, help us to survive the dark side of love,
the dark moments of marriage. Make us be
patient and forgive each other's faults.
Every day may not be beautiful, but every day
will have something of love in it.
Do not let either one of us walk on eggshells
or want the last word all the time. When
the storm of anger is over, let us wait
patiently for the sun to shine again,
know that we belong together forever.

—*Marion Schoeberlein*

Spouses' Prayer for Each Other

Dear God,
grant that I and my spouse may have a true
and understanding love for each other.
Grant that we may both
be filled with faith and trust.
Give us the grace to live
with each other in peace and harmony.
May we always bear with each other's weaknesses
and grow from each other's strengths.
Help us to forgive each other's failings
and grant us patience, kindness, cheerfulness,
and the spirit of placing the well-being
of each other ahead of self.

May the love that brought us together
grow and mature with each passing year.
Bring us both ever closer to You
through our love for each other.
Let our love grow to perfection.

Amen.

—*Author unknown*

Prayer of the Military Wife

Dear God, I am proud to be wed to one who defends freedom and peace. My challenges are many and I pray for Your love and guidance to meet them. Special to me are the symbols representing my religion, country, community, and home. I pray for the wisdom and grace to be true to their meanings. You are the symbol of my religious beliefs and the source of my strength. Because my life is full of change, I cherish the solid and constant spiritual foundation that You provide. Help me, Lord, to be an example of Your teachings. My national flag represents freedom. Let me never forget, or take for granted, the hope it shows to the world. Bless those who have made sacrifices for freedom.

Please grant us Your continued blessings, increased strength, and infinite guidance as we live to Your honor and glory. Amen.

—*Author unknown*

Our Bond

When life moves us
away from each other
and we fail to remember
our delight in each other's laughter,
the way our bodies suit
and complement each other,
times when we lifted
and held each other during storms
of need, disappointment, and loss,
strengthen our bond, Lord,
lest we forget
the love You gave us.

—*Shirley Kobar*

Expanding Hearts

Give us expanding hearts, Holy Creating Love,
hearts that can take in all the beauty
> of the persons we love,
> expanding to the full scope of their becoming,
> extending through their time and space
> > to welcome all they are and will become,
> > their blossoming,
> > > trials,
> > > and full growth,
> > > even their diminishment and death.

That is the lovingness to which we are called.
Grace us with hearts for love's entire journey,
> from mysterious sunrise
> to mysterious sunset.

Amen.

—*William Cleary*

Living Realistically

Lord, teach us both to live realistically, to face life with gut-level honesty. God, give us the levelheadedness to accept failure, irritations, even anguish, as part and parcel of our spiritual growth. Help us to recognize that disagreements and differences are included in our family heritage. Remind us often that contentment is a blessing, not a contract; that emptying the trash or cleaning an oven creates more friction than fun, that a cold shower minus a song doesn't always indicate regression. At least once in a while, dear Lord, we ought to be able to give vent to our moods without one of us suggesting personal counseling. Too often we cling to our storybook dream of living happily ever after. It will come true, Lord. But only in the home You've prepared for us. Until then, give us the maturity to accept and the willingness to wait.

—*Johanna D. Spangenberg*

Generosity of Spirit

There are times
I stubbornly
insist upon my will and way,
disregarding
the preferences and needs
of my partner and mate.
Bless us with generosity
of spirit and patience
to halt our inconsiderate endeavors;
hasty, hurtful words,
and see You
in the face of our beloved.

—*Shirley Kobar*

Marriage as Prayer

May your marriage be a prayer
that you offer to God
with open hearts
full of devotion.
May it glorify Him
and bring you a peace
that never ceases,
a strength that the world
cannot diminish.

—*Darrell Lindsey*

2

⁊

Blessings

Blessing

May goodness ever surround you,
may grace keep its arms around you.
May God, rich in mercy,
grant that you'll be
filled with all the love your
heart can hold
and every road
bring you together.

May distance not separate you
while oceans and stars await you.
May what you have tasted
not be wasted
in the turning of the
potter's wheel.
It's turning still.
You are together.

May Christ be ever before you
and in time of need restore you.
May Christ be within you,
may He win you
ever more through each new
night and day
and guide your way
into together.

—Jim Croegaert

A Blessing Fair

Dear Lord,
Bless our union,
fill it with your will.
Temper our disagreements,
with forgiveness,
our touches with compassion,
and our children,
with lovingness.

—*Michael Young*

A Blessing for the Newly Married

May you be companions
in the complexity of lived lives.

May your days dance
like crystals in sunlight

as you celebrate the birth of all
that is beautiful and unexpected and new.

May your names be a song
on each other's lips

and each breath remind you
that the bread you share

comes from the earth
which bonds us all, sisters, brothers . . .

And when you return home
each evening, may you find there

a Sabbath of rest and peace,
where you are free to choose

the place of your own kneeling,
where you worship at the edge

of each other's open door.

—*Michael S. Glaser*

Ever Growing

Dear Newlyweds,

May you always worship God together,
never worship yourselves or each other.

May you always remember your good times
and forget every hard, sad, bad time.

Let your love be spoken true and often
in words as well as in faithful action.

May you enjoy many common interests,
yet appreciate your differences.

May you learn to sleep soundly together,
ever growing in trust of each other.

—*Marjorie Gray*

The Blessing of Yes

Borrow only the smallest threads
as you enter the sacred arc of marriage.
Love, hope, friends, and family surround
you as you begin to weave the tapestry
of your lives together. Gather all you
have been given, all you have learned,
all you have to offer each other
into bold patterns, stars of light,
crimsons and greens, and flowers
of comfort. Let your stitches be fine
and surely knotted. For the tapestry
of *yes,* borrow only the smallest threads.

For your blue, you need neither garter,
glove, nor thread, nor powdery ribbon.
Take what lies before you—the sky,
the river, the fullness of days ahead.
Paint a canopy across your horizon,
indigo for the blessings of family,
yellow for the laughter of friends,
rose for your home and children to come.
Use a swath of brightest red for your
courage to commit two lives forever.
May prisms of light dance in your honor
in the blue just beneath the sun.

For what is old, take with you only
what is treasured. For the rest, old
loneliness, worries, complexities—
let them circle, sway, fall away.
Your roots are entwined with wisdom
and values of those who have taught
you well. Let faith in what you know
guide you and deepen your love for this
world and each other. Your rings will
will gather luster as you hold each other
through laughter and the giddy promise
of youth, through sleepless nights
and sorrows sure to come. Be comforted
by old treasures as well as the new.

And for new, what do you need but this—
What you have, may it increase.
What you bring, may you share gladly.
What you have left behind, let it rest.
What you must learn, may you learn it
together and joyfully. May this covenant
bind you with the balm of delight,
the grace of each other's gaze, and may
it blaze with the warmth of having found,
each in the other, a brilliant new blessing.

                    Yes.

—*Davi Walders*

The Wonder of Your Being

May your days be made full
with the wonder of your being,
the wonder of each other
and your lives upon this earth.
May your days be made full
with the wonder of existence
of the earth amid the stars,
the stars amid the heavens,
and the heavens within your hearts.

—*Ingrid Goff-Maidoff*

Seven Wedding Blessings

Because you have chosen a life together,
  May your joy deepen
  May your wisdom increase
  May your passion for life and each other intensify
  May your compassion for yourselves and others
    expand
  May your support and gentleness toward each other
    grow
  May your generosity to yourselves, each other, and
    your community be enhanced
  May goodness abide with you always and may you
    flourish and prosper together.

—*Davi Walders*

Divine Wisdom, Eternal Love

Divine Wisdom, Eternal Love,
Guide these two on their journey together.
Keep them faithful and strong,
able to bend like pines before the wind.
Give them the wings of love
to rise above petty differences.
And keep a song in their hearts.
Let them witness life's beautiful radiance
as the sun rises in the morning
for another day of joy.
And give them many moons
and stars to count their blessings by.

—*Ingrid Goff-Maidoff*

The Safe Harbor

May God bless your marriage with a safe harbor, a place deep enough and wide enough to stay through the storms. May God make your marriage a map for exploring and a garden for growing. May God grace you with a heart to encourage each other and a laugh to enjoy each other, and may God give you the grace to be fools for each other.

—*Martha K. Baker*

Hand in Hand

Under the canopy of your heavens
before friends and neighbors
we profess our love
and dedicate ourselves to You.
In joy and sorrow
gift us with Your presence.
Bless us as we walk
hand in hand on Your path.

—*Shirley Kobar*

3

Toasts

Toast to You and Me

May we honor always the unique I
of each other
as we accept now the sacred vow of creating
an eternal WE.
May our love be as wide as the prairie skies,
as luminous as the wings of the dragonfly,
as tenacious and enduring as the blue-green lichen
that blooms on stone.
May the power of our love
illuminate life's humble minutes,
its peak moments and all the nows between.

—*Susan J. Erickson*

A Toast to Our Family and Friends

We are gathered here to share
the joy of our decision to love each other.
We are here with those who started this love story—
    you.
You showed us the meaning of the word *love* in your
    everyday actions.
We are here because of you.

—*Zoraida Rivera Morales*

Tender Toast

Joining hands, joining hearts.
Pledging love, promising laughter.
A song, a sigh of sentiment.
A toast, a treasure, time, and tenderness.
A wedding, a whisper of wonderment.
A dance, a dream, a destiny.
Memories to be written in the stars,
Lyrics to be lived in everlasting love.
Blessings to you both, now and always.

—*Judith A. Lindberg*

Ingredients of a Happy Marriage

May your disagreements be quickly resolved,
your shared interests many,
your commitment never failing,
and your loyalty enduring.

May you both be more give than take,
may your marriage be your top priority,
may your love be strong,
and your happiness eternal.

—*Katherine Swarts*

A Newlywed's Toast

May today's love burn brightly,
may tomorrow's love polish your lives,
and many years from now,
may your hearts be warmed
    by the glow of a flame
    that never died.

—*Sally Clark*

A Toast to the Newlyweds

May your sunny smiles capture your love and hold it
  close for safekeeping,
May your vows sharpen and deepen with time, and
  may time be kind to you,
May today's grace visit in mundane moments when
  you toast a common good,
And when this world tilts, may you find peaceful
  balance in each other's love.

—*Martha K. Baker*

Shine Always

May the love that lives within your eyes today
shine always, like a lighthouse built on rock—
strong and secure in spite of heavy weather—
a beacon in the dark that endures and welcomes home.

—*Candy Killion*

4

Daily Life

Sunrise

Now is the sunrise of our love.

As our days unfold before us,
bless us with friendship, patience, and understanding,
      for without these, love cannot endure.

Bless us with courtesy, kindness, and compassion for
      each other,
            for without these, love cannot flourish.

Bless us with laughter and tears, toil and fun,
      for without these, love cannot grow.

May we live together,
      love together,
      grow together,
      be together,

from the sunrise of our love
until the sunset of our lives.

—*Sandra E. McBride*

Listening

Listening is a talent,
perfected by practice,
not easily acquired.
It's so much more
than simply waiting
for your turn to speak.

Listening is a decision,
a willing choice made
to hear beyond the words,
peer behind the eyes,
tune in to the unspoken.

Listening without trying
to change or fix another
hovers somewhere between
artistry and therapy.

So don't ponder
on the perfect response
to fix others, but try,
instead, to hear what
they're not saying.

—*Susan R. Norton*

For Those Times Spent Apart

Know that time spent apart
does not ever separate two hearts
joined in joyful, sacred union.
The geography of such love
is comforting and beautiful:
Where one goes
the other's spirit goes also.
You have surely sensed
this nearness of your beloved
in times of absence—
had your feelings defy distance and days.
May you cling to the cheerful fact
that your beloved's arms
are always embracing you,
as are God's.

—*Darrell Lindsey*

The Excitable Gift

Half awake,
I smell
the coffee brewing
in the kitchen,
and the sunlight is
spilling across
the hardwood floor,
and it is
Saturday morning
and I have
no place
to hurry
out of bed for
except
to eat
breakfast
with the one
I love.

—*Mike W. Blottenberger*

Too often we underestimate the power of a touch, a smile, a kind word, a listening ear, an honest compliment, or the smallest act of caring, all of which have the potential to turn life around.

—Leo Buscaglia (1924–1998)

Love Comes First

Though there will be moments of hurt,
times of emotional pain,
days when communication may not be possible,
let us always put love first.

And, during the times of sharing and laughter,
let's remember to tell each other
how good it is between us.

I will never be too busy to listen,
so ask, anytime, for any reason.
I'll be honest and I'll be here
with love.

—*Judith A. Lindberg*

When Love Is Painful

Holy mystery of love,
as we give thanks for Your presence
when love flows like a river,
so we are grateful for Your presence
when love refuses to flow,
when love is slogging work,
and even when love is painful.

It is still love, and it is still charged with Your energies.

You inspire us to make our love ever wider,
to open its doors even to the woundedness
of those we love,
to admit honestly to our own wounds
and defective hearts,
to patiently allow time to pass: for healing.

Love can be lost we know, Holy One,
and we ask Your blessing on what love we have.

Even though it be imperfect,
still it towers over everything else in our life.

Amen.

—*William Cleary*

Why Do I Love You?

Is it snuggling in front of a roaring fire
that makes me love you so?
Or strolling in the woods among dormant trillium
beneath the melted snow?
Is it admiring the sunset over the pond
while you stand beside me close?
Or biking on a lazy Sunday afternoon
down dusty country roads?
Is it the way we share, or care,
or bare our souls to bind our hearts?
Or is it simply because you're a gift from God
and we promised never to part?

—Donna Wyland

A Promise

When tears are not enough to wash away the pain,
you are there to comfort me.

When happiness shines on my life, waiting to be
    shared,
you are there to dance with me.

When worries fill my mind and wear away my
    confidence,
you are there to listen to me.

Things will change as time goes on;
there will be different sorrows,
different worries,
different moments of joy.

Just know in your heart,
through good and through bad,
I will be here for you.

—*Andrea L. Mack*

Your Song

Your song sings always in me
even when you are silent,
even when you are away.
To me there is no sound
as soft as you,
no voice on earth
that gives my feet
such wings,
no whispered prayer
filled with so much promise.
Your voice is the pillow
on which I rest my heart,
the blanket with which
I warm my dreams,
the bed in which my soul
learns its nightly lesson
of everlasting love.

—*Charles Ghigna*

Keep Your Dwelling Strong

Keep your dwelling strong,
each a shelter for the other.
Keep your dwelling peaceful,
a place to rest and be inspired.
Keep your dwelling beautiful;
see the sacred in all things.
May all who come to see you
know they visit a house of love.

Keep your dwelling simple,
not to crowd out essential things.
Keep harmony in your dwelling
by sharing a common dream.
Guard each other's solitude,
that neither becomes lost to the Self.
And be good company to each other,
that neither feels alone.

—*Ingrid Goff-Maidoff*

Mask

You see through my mask.
You feel my frustration
and sense the warmth
of tears flowing freely
in the wake of my smile
as if they were your own.

You see through my mask.
You pardon my uncertainty
and understand crippling fears
that take their hold
as courage wanes,
for they have been your own.

You remove my mask,
revealing a power
that lies beneath imagined weakness,
and at that moment
I become aware
that together we are strength.

—*Monica E. Smith*

Windy Afternoon

It is a windy afternoon, and we are in love,
the currents of invisible energies
    ruffling our hair,
    making us smile.

You are here, invisible God, on every side,
    touching us though we cannot feel your touch,
    laughing with us though we hear nothing—
    because your touch and your laugh are so
    continuous
        we have long ago stopped noticing them.

Every detail of our being and our being in love
    contains your spirit,
and we know that—
    because the whole scene is unexplainable
        without your empowerment.

Hear our human word of thanks.

Amen.

—*William Cleary*

So Many Things

How is it
you always
get me to do
so many things
I would not do
without you,
so many things
that take us
out of ourselves
and bring us back
a little closer,
so many things
our separate hearts
would not have known,
would not have loved,
alone.

—*Charles Ghigna*

Few Words

Some evenings
   few words
      pass between us.

You may be
   reading the paper
      or a new book,

and I may be
   planning a new lesson
      or writing a poem.

These are activities
   we could do
      in separate rooms,

yet the void
   created when
      we're apart

is too distracting.

—*David B. McCoy*

Lessons

It is in the very act
of loving each other
day by day
with patience
with humor
with doubts
with passion
and much forgiveness,
all without losing ourselves,
that we learn to love.

—*Arlene Gay Levine*

*Two are better off than one, because together
they can work more effectively. If one of them
falls down, the other can help him up.*

—*Ecclesiastes 4:9–10 (GNT)*

More Than One Plus One

Sometimes it will seem
there's suddenly too much to carry—
that one plus one
has quickly added up
to more than four hands can juggle.
Yet sometimes it will be
when your hands are busiest
that you will find them the stronger
when you choose to leave them open, to welcome
and hold the love that brought you here.

—*Peg Duthie*

Attraction

The feeling I had today,
while sitting across from you,
was pure magnetism.

It was to have the randomly
aligned magnetic domains
of my being suddenly turned

in one direction and
attracted to your love.

—David B. McCoy

Prayer After a Quarrel

Today, reality and expectation
didn't match;
we quarreled
when we most wanted
to be close.

Lord,
help us listen more
and say less.
Help us avoid
reaching conclusions
before we hear
what the other has to say.

Make us slow to anger
and quick to make up.
Teach us to remember
we can't read
each other's mind.

Lord, keep loving us
unconditionally.
Teach us to keep on loving
every day—
as we discover once again
who we are.

—*Zoraida Rivera Morales*

Recording Joy

You may think you'll recall
the excitement,
the newness,
the change—
as though everything
happened yesterday.

But time will pass,
and you'll soon ask,
"When did we go to—?"
or "Where did we buy—?"
or "What was that
family's name?"

From the beginning,
make personal notes
and hoard mementos.
They'll help you relive
today's joys again
and again, together.

—*Joanne Keaton*

On the Road

The road of marriage
has hills and valleys,
mountains and oceans
to see and explore.

Be sure to carry in your backpack
the water of love,
enough understanding to feed you both,
the glasses of faithfulness,
the medicine of God's word,
and a new pair of shoes,
laced with sincerity
and constructed with trust.

—*Zoraida Rivera Morales*

Devoted

My heart can be your home.
My soul can be your refuge.
You can turn to me when you are weak.
You can call to me when the way is not clear.
I will be your promise, your prayer, and I
will always be there.
Constant, complete.
Run to me, reach out for me, and I will love
you in a unique and tender way.
Bring your love to me.
Share your love with me.
Sing your love to me, and I will give you
peace, ease, and comfort.

—*Lori Eberhardy*

5

Romance

Starshine

Your touch is always present
like the wind upon my face.
I listen for your laughter,
I long for your embrace.

All my dreams are given wings,
my mind is free from fear,
the days are full of happiness
because your love is near.

You light my path on darkest nights,
you show me that you care,
my courage has no limits
as long as you are there.

Somewhere it's written in the stars,
I feel it in my heart;
we are meant to share our lives
and never be apart.

I put no faith in chance or fate
but seek the higher view;
I believe there is a God—
because He gave me you.

—*C. David Hay*

The Love Within

I am here to love you with an open heart.

If my arms were filled with stars,
when I released them they would echo my love
as they fell around your feet.

If I could hold the warmth of the sun in my pocket,
I would share it with you
when your heart needed a warm embrace.

And if I had the power
to make all your dreams come true,
I would give you days filled with
beautiful treasure, gentle surprises, and pure joy.

So as I wrap my arms around you
know that you are never beyond my love.

—*Lori Eberhardy*

How beautiful you are, my love; how your eyes shine with love!

—Song of Solomon 1:15 (GNT)

Like God, Perhaps

The face of my love
is etched with images
I am awed by
again and again.

She has measured
the waters of my soul
and surely
has found me wanting;

yet look:

she loves me,
she loves me.

—*Michael S. Glaser*

Commitment

We stood like two trees
   in a fairy tale, leaning
   toward each other in the night . . .
   Our dreams went up into the sky
   and became stars . . .
   Our hearts smiled in the dark
   and we knew that love was
   even more beautiful
   at night than in the day . . .

—*Marion Schoeberlein*

Easter Sunday

When I say, I love you,
even after these ten months,
and at least ten times a day,
it leaves my mouth like a prayer.

And as strong as any faith
I've had in anything,
I know our love is guided
by a heavenly power which—
despite having once been
lost or beaten down—
has risen again within our hearts.

—*David B. McCoy*

The Terms of Love

When
we finally
turned to
each other
after the chase,
every part
of my being
cried out,
"Surrender."

—*Joan Noëldechen*

You are like a dove that hides in the crevice
of a rock. Let me see your lovely face
and hear your enchanting voice.

—Song of Solomon 2:14 (GNT)

When the Acacia Blooms

bees go crazy, get drunk on the honey-soaked air.
I think I could sit here forever, inhaling this sweetness,

thinking about the time we sat in sunlight filtered by
   its twice-compound leaves, in some small village in
   France, the name now

faded ink on the back of a snapshot. What I remember
   is the sun,
how it licked our arms and faces like a rough-tongued
   cat,

how everything was aureate that spring afternoon,
like walking into a painting; how we shared

a sandwich, *jambon et fromage,* your hand covered mine,
and I thought of the night before, our small room,

how we climbed the ladder of each other's body until
   the stars
showered us with sparks, and then we fell. . . .

Where today, this scent of wisteria, purple racemes
   falling
from twisted vines reminds me of acacia in the warm
   April sun,

so thick you could spread it on toast or bottle it in glass
   jars. Off
in the distance, doves call, their long vowels not
   mournful but one

of those sounds that taps into memory's underground
   river, this waterfall
of flowers, pouring its hot breath onto the stunned air.

—*Barbara Crooker*

Carefree

Enraptured
with the joy
of being two,
bicycling
on a country road
near sunset
on a summer's night.

—*Susan Landon*

Our Hands

Our hands intertwine
like two small birds
nestling close,
keeping warm in each
other's down feathers.

Our hands, like sparrows,
sing without words,
for music so eloquent
doesn't need words.

—*Ida Fasel*

Moments to Remember

Do you remember
our first kiss—
the moment my lips
barely brushed yours?

Oh, how my heart danced,
nearly leaped
through my chest,
pounding with desire.

I remember,
and on each occasion
love you more.

—*Mary Lenore Quigley*

The Religion of
Everyday Things

We return at nightfall, shoulders bowed, weighed down
by slights and insults. They fall from us at the door,

as everything beyond these walls recedes. The horns
and sirens, the pain and desperation that invade our
    outside

life: all are silenced. We join each other and sit,
and rise and sit, in unison. Then, cleansed, we bow our
    heads,

letting love seep over the table until even the most
    humble
foods—the potatoes, the salt—feel shy and deeply
    cherished.

When the meal ends, we find that we are pulled apart
strand by strand, that the walls and floor are as deeply
    connected

as our arms and legs. The elements have to weave
and reweave as we move from room to room, sitting
    down in one

or walking out of another. We connect almost as fluidly,
    bashful
as strangers. Courteous, we pass in the hallways without
    touching;

we close each door with the faintest sound; we say
   please
and *thank you* and *God bless you*, again and again, as
   though the act

of sneezing were a form of prayer and we were only
   answering
in kind. In silence, we perform the ritual ablutions, as
   we always

have: bathing in the dim sunlight of the morning,
   washing our faces
as we undress for bed. And in the end we lift the quilts
   and find

each other there, waiting, every breath reverent,
every touch of skin a testament.

—*Leah Browning*

6

∽

Intimacy

I Wanted to Tell You

I wanted to tell you how,
early this morning

lying against you,
a great wave of gentleness

swept all my old wars
clean, leaving me here with

your body washed up in sleep
on the pillow beside me.

I am here, home,
and empty of all but your deep

silence humming within me.
I wanted to tell you

I love you.

—*Marjorie Rommel*

Lazy Morning Love

My eyes crawl slowly up the sheets,
striving to memorize each nook and cranny
of a body that cocoons the man I love.

They search out your head, half secreted
beneath the bed pillow, then strike out
to graze your slightly bearded cheek.

I try to memorize each tweak of an eyelid,
the quake of a lip, the whiff of a smile.

I snuggle up to your sleep-warmed form,
sink into the sensation of skin on skin,
applaud your scent, anticipate each breath,
attempt to match mine to yours and
try to join with you in your dream.

—Susan R. Norton

Pillow Talk

Help us remember that our love reflects the love of
  God.
We look at each other. Our pulses race.
We turn down the lights, turn down the sheets,
approach our bed together.
Bless us in the sacredness of this intimate time together.
May we be faithful and loving friends,
compassionate and tender now and always
in all the ways we are together.
May we know each other's deepest name.

—*Linda Goodman Robiner*

*Husbands, love your wives just as Christ
loved the church and gave his life for it.*

—Ephesians 5:25 (GNT)

This Morning

I awaken again warm,
my body pressed against his
spoon-fashion,
as if one.

We didn't start our sleep that way.
We're never aware of the change.

It must be a quiet yearning for touch
that creeps into the subconscious,
drawing us together in the dark
unencumbered hours of slumber.

I lie unmoving,
unthinking, really,
simply enjoying again
his smell, his quiet breath,
him.

Thank you, God.

—*Barbara J. Mitchell*

So Much for Chores

The kitchen radio rumbles heavy drumbeat,
outside, rain pecks out its staccato
on the porch.
Stirring fragrant coffee,
I ponder doing dishes, starting laundry,
pause to glance at him.
Across from me,
his eye-crinkling smile
liquefies all my resolve.
Oh, listen,
to that insistent rain
and heartbeats drumming.

—Sara Sanderson

Journey

Afterward, I almost do
but decide not to try to
think of a word
to describe it. Just be
quiet. Rest at the edge
of pleasure, the beyond
our bodies enter into.
Burrow my head between
his neck and his shoulder.
Accept that my breath just
spiraled out and will spiral
back down into me slowly.

How far out I unravel.
How far away from ourselves
and how deep into ourselves
we travel when we travel that
way—through one another.
As though we feed one hunger
with two bodies.
Even knowing better that
we are separate hungers
feeding the one body
our bodies become.

—*Marylisa W. DeDomenicis*

The Greatest Day

they all said it would be the greatest day of my life;
they were wrong
today is better—
waking to the sleeping nuzzle
   of his stubbled chin
the rise and fall of his rhythmed breath
the playful splay of his hair on rumpled cotton
the gentle rest of his fingers on my hip
   watching him till he wakes
and smiles at the sight of his love
pulling me closer,
   my husband

—*AJ Kallies*

Bedground

I snake my legs
   around yours
or burrow
like a prairie dog
into the warmth
beneath your side,
seeking,
in the mindlessness
of midnight, the still
unconscious comfort
of your sleeping form.

—*Maureen Tolman Flannery*

River

I used to swim in crystal
streams that pour their clarity
over the mountains,
but I didn't understand.

Then you came like an answer
to the impossible burning
prayer of my being—
Know me.

Now we dive deep
wild waters of the heart
and boundaries blur
in the shimmering river.

—Kathy Conde

Married . . .

Does my mate know
I like the scent
of his hair, or I
sometimes still hug
folded laundry ready
to touch his skin?
Watching his morning
shave elicits smiles,
while his nighttime
breathing sound
makes me feel safe.
He's my closest friend,
and the one who
listens to my
quiet whispers.

—*Lois Greene Stone*

Yellow Linens

As we lie in our bed today,
covered in yellow linens
scented with rose sachet,
I slip back to remember
it was only yesterday, when
we looked out the narrow window
with its shutters opened wide.

The wind blew over our shadows
as I shivered by your side.
You whispered, "*I'll keep you warm,*"
then wrapped the top sheet
over my nude form.

I didn't understand this
was not pretend, but love's
natural command.
Just as nature sends the lily
to lie beneath a blanket of snow
certain its fragrant flower will bloom
as the springtime rain seeps low.

We, too, are part of this intricate plan
as we lie upon our yellow bed
thinking of how it all began—
when fellowship intimate, visited
eyes beholding genuine love,
our souls intertwined.

—*Susan Fridkin*

Loving

When a couple discovers
the passion of their love
they feel pleasure and unity.

When a couple learns
to love each other with passion
they feel the magnitude
of God's love.

—*Zoraida Rivera Morales*

Midnight Wandering

I like to feel your body twitch
and hear your breathing grow more audible
as you slide into sleep between my shoulder
and your unremembered dreams.
There's a cobweb in the corner that I missed
and a mystery grease spot on the ceiling.
The intermittent furnace start-ups
alternate with my stomach growls.

In this stillness of almost midnight,
in this love of almost always,
I imagine how a mother feels
with a child in her arms.
I wish I had known you
when you were a boy.
I missed so much.
Did you have freckles?
Can my love insinuate its joy into your past?

The streetlight glare through lacy curtains
enlivens the spirals of this old iron bed.
Now angels, now monsters of the deep
share my watch.
I must
wake you
to tell of my love,
or perhaps because my arm has gone to sleep.

—*Maureen Tolman Flannery*

Dreaming Awake

Morning, and already
I see your soft image
take shape inside
my sleepy mind.
But it is not until
you stir beside me
that I know the
joy of waking,
that I know it is time
to open my eyes
and dream.

—*Charles Ghigna*

7

Reflections

Love

To trust in what I
do not understand—

The way flowers follow
with imperceptible grace
the sequence of day,

to bend at nightfall
like wheat in the wind,

to let go
like seedpods
anticipating spring,

to be still
with the softness
of my body, breathing,

is to be, perhaps,
like prayer

alive
and vital in the air.

—*Michael S. Glaser*

On Marriage

The marriage road is full of bumps
with many stones along the path,
some small enough to pick up
and lightly toss aside,
others heavy as boulders—
each one a burden to weigh you down
until you carry it to the next clearing,
sometimes miles away—
but if you walk together,
mindful of the rocky places,
though you may stumble you will not fall
into the traps that lie hidden in the shadows.

—*Rosalie Calabrese*

Lasting Love

When the first wave of passion has faded,
remember that love need not die.
Nothing keeps its fresh flavor forever,
but much will grow purer with time.

When the cheese has grown ripe and less mellow,
the flavor has joys of its own.
When the wine has grown old in the cellar,
its truest appeal can be known.

And so is it when love has grown purer:
when fresh, it seems all life can give,
but when it has been nurtured for decades,
it's only beginning to live.

—*Katherine Swarts*

You Complete Me

Somehow,
you complete me,
as if
    a piece
        of the puzzle
            called Me
has always been missing,
and I didn't know how much
    I needed it,
        until I met you.

—*Susan R. Norton*

Homecoming

You have awakened
in me senses I had not known.
You have discovered
my inmost nature,
impenetrable until now,
and scaled the walls
of my heart to rest
in my soul. Do you find it
warm and familiar?
It is because here
you have always existed,
destined to dwell.
You filled the emptiness in my life
long before I knew you,
and now, at long last,
you have revealed yourself—
Welcome home!

—*Monica E. Smith*

Husband Song

I would be with you
in old age.
I would be tenderly wiping
the milk from your fierce gray beard,
holding your arm as we cross the street
slowly.

I would be with you
in old age,
saving you from sitting alone
like the men you saw through lit doorways
off the dark corridors
of the houses where you lived.

We will rock together on some porch
whose posts are twined with morning glory,
whistling bird calls into the night.

—*Penny Harter*

A good woman is hard to find, and worth
far more than diamonds. Her husband
trusts her without reserve, and never
has reason to regret it.

—*Proverbs 31:10–11 (The Message)*

Kismet

Before I knew who you were
I loved you,
never wanting more.
Never settling for less.
Knowing you were out there,
somewhere.
Your essence, your being
caressed me, cloaked me, invited me
to look for and find you
faithfully, fatefully following
that uphill winding path
that would inevitably lead me,
persuade me, and
coax me to that place
where you would find me;
finding you.

—*Robin Svedi*

Until one is committed, there is hesitancy, the chance to draw back, always ineffectiveness. Concerning all acts of initiation (and creation), there is one elementary truth, the ignorance of which kills countless ideas and splendid plans: that the moment one definitely commits oneself, then Providence moves, too. All sorts of things occur to help one that would never otherwise have occurred. A whole stream of events issues from the decision, raising in one's favor all manner of unforeseen incidents and meetings and material assistance which no man could have dreamed would have come his way. Whatever you can do or dream you can, begin it. Boldness has genius, power, and magic in it. Begin it now.

Attributed to Johann Wolfgang von Goethe (1749–1832)

The Light at the End of the Street

On a dark rural road that is devoid of streetlights, the houses have plenty of breathing room. But one lonely porch light reaches into the night. Someone is waiting for you to come home from the overtime, the gym, the grocery store. A light is glowing in the darkness—it's a love thing.

—*Jodi M. Webb*

Combinations

There is a combination for everything—
the way I wear my hair
and you yours,
my squint
and your wide-open stare.
The combination
of words put to paper,
the combination
of words that never appear.

The Universe
combines us,
and we commingle with the stars—
the way a comet passes its years
out there,
the way we pass ours
here.

—Julia Older

Do Good Things
for Each Other

Do good things for each other—
small kindnesses every day.
Be a comfort to each other—
a calm shore in turbulent times.

Be good friends to each other—
remain compassionate and tender.
Lend a thoughtful ear, a gentle shoulder,
an open heart, and a strong hand.

And do good things for each other.

—Ingrid Goff-Maidoff

Hands

When love seizes
your hand, it's gently meant
to keep you from a fall,
promising,
when harder times come,
as they so often do,
his good hand will not fail
as long as yours is there
to hold you both secure.

—*Ida Fasel*

Honeymoon

On our honeymoon
we traveled from place to place.
I would wake in the night,
forgetting what city I was in,
what room surrounded me,
what season it was.
I patted the bed on my right
to be sure you were beside me.

Now as we journey from place
to place in our married life
I awake in the night
and wonder what stage we are in now,
what season is just turning,
what future surrounds us.
I pat the bed on my right.
You are still beside me.

—*Donna Wahlert*

The Language of Love

A simple touch, a hand gently stroking her hair, the look that is a secret language between two souls, it is the heart reaching out, longing to give to another, to fulfill its destiny, its irresistible urge. We all long to be loved, but perhaps even more strongly we long to love. To give ourselves without condition to another. To see only their soul and the divine within.

To love is to look beyond the world and for that moment be transported into a world where there is nothing but you and your beloved. Where your soul leaps for joy and the longings of your heart are heard. The soul longs to speak, to give another person the safe space to speak their truth, that is truly love.

—*Erica Staab Westmoreland*

Thank You

Thank you for this man,
his eyes eager with hope,
who by Your hand chose me as
his love,
his partner,
his wife.
Thank you for the chance
to share of my heart,
to become one of two,
for now and for always.
Thank you for
Your precious gift.

—*Michelle Close Mills*

You Are Mine, I Am Yours

You are mine.
I am yours.
Not a possessive noun
that expresses property,
but a meaningful word
declaring our decision
to share the best we have—
to listen, to honor,
to understand,
to cheer each other,
to love each other,
being who we are.

You are mine.
I am yours.
Together life is lovelier.

—*Zoraida Rivera Morales*

When Death Will
Come to Part Us

When death will come to part us
let us be thankful that
God blessed our lives with so much love.
If I go first, pray that my spirit
remembers you always with joy.
Let me dance in heaven when I think of you,
and if I am the one left here alone,
wish happiness for me in all the memories you left,
beauty in every day, friends and family still here.
Let me not mourn, knowing you are with God
and I will come someday to be with you again.

—*Marion Schoeberlein*

Our Marriage

Woman,
      You are mine to hold,
      all the beauty and joy
      of the red rose.
      A treasure to cherish
      and press between
      the pages
      in the book of my life
      and you are beloved.

Man,
      You are as precious
      as the gold ring I will wear,
      an unending circle of love
      expanding my world
      like widening ripples
      in a pool when
      a pebble is dropped.
      You are at the center
      of all that is
      blessed in my life
      and we are one.

—Beatrice O'Brien

A Mystery

How two imperfect humans can meet, marry, and get along well is perhaps a mystery to man and God.

—*Norma Woodbridge*

Our Lives

You sleep, I dream,
imagining tomorrow
and all the tomorrows
of our life.

Will we have children,
change jobs,
buy a house in the suburbs,
have outdoor barbeques?

Perhaps we'll stay in the city,
live in a loft,
decorate in bold colors,
and ride our bikes to work.

You sleep, I dream,
imagining tomorrow
and all the tomorrows
of our love.

—*Eve Lomoro*

8

Inspiration

Between You and Me

You are here inside my laughter.
Thoughts of you are on my mind and
wrapped around my heart.
You empower me to love with all I have,
and to enjoy all that is good.
As I embrace each day with the promise of you,
I can't imagine a day that is not filled
with your smiles.
My life has been kissed by many blessings,
and because of you each day is a gift
filled with grace, mercy, and love.
I cherish the moments that bring us together,
and it is inside this space I realize I am home.

—Lori Eberhardy

Changing Directions

Enclosed in your warmth
    I have felt free
        to run
           to the limits
of my possibilities.
        You helped to release in me
              this river of feeling
          in which I am no longer drowning
            but swimming
                toward
                    tomorrow.

—*Molly Srode*

Together Forever

1. We shall love and be faithful to each other.
2. We shall honor the holy bonds of matrimony.
3. We shall show steadfast love and not take each other for granted.
4. We shall be tolerant and forgiving of each other.
5. We shall do our labors and be aware of each other's needs and desires.
6. We shall teach our children the importance of God, living and loving by our example.
7. We shall honor our parents.
8. We shall not say or do unkind things. God planned marriage to be a duet, not a duel.
9. We shall throw the word *divorce* out of our vocabulary so it cannot be used in anger.
10. We shall strive to make our marriage a haven for us, a very special and secure relationship.

—*Phyllis Joy Davison*

The Journey's Start

Here we are, at our beginning,
looking into each other's eyes,
so full of love, so full of dreams,
and I am happy to share it all,
with you.

—*Michael Young*

Love is patient; love is kind; love is not
envious or boastful or arrogant or rude.
It does not insist on its own way; it is not
irritable or resentful; it does not rejoice in
wrongdoing, but rejoices in the truth.
It bears all things, believes all things,
hopes all things, endures all things.

—1 Corinthians 13:4–7 (NRSV)

Keep the Joy

Hold tight to the old-fashioned notion
that love doesn't have to lose its glow—
the glow your face showed and your heart knew
when you first kissed your beloved's lips.
Keep that joy by being kind to each other,
forgiving of faults—
trying always to understand the other's needs.
Keep that warmth and peace of spirit
by sharing hopes and dreams;
by soaring together day by day.
Know that God surely smiles
upon such a selfless sky.

—*Darrell Lindsey*

When the Future Has Come and Gone

When the future has come and gone,
when the lessons of life are through,
the greatest joy for me will be
knowing I was loved by you.

—*Susan R. Norton*

Immutable Star

It takes a rare person to care the way you do.
When I want someone to hold me, there you are.
The things I'm learning from you help me
handle my tasks confidently.
You listen even when it means giving
time you need for yourself.
If I am feeling blue, you know a way to make me laugh.
Sometimes all I require is to hear your voice
or see you smile and I find my way again.
Your belief in my abilities is a guide through tough times
and spurs me on when I must challenge myself.
You recognize my weaknesses as opportunities
for growth; my accomplishments are cause
for you to celebrate. Respecting our separate
identities you nourish our bond.
Setting sail on this journey together, I have no fear,
for your love is the immutable star
by which I'll steer my life.

—*Arlene Gay Levine*

Place me like a seal over your heart,
like a seal on your arm;
for love is as strong as death,
its jealousy unyielding as the grave.
It burns like blazing fire,
like a mighty flame.

—Song of Solomon 8:6 (NIV)

Beloved

My soul quietly flows into you,
and as you lead me to your gentle embrace,
I exhale and welcome the peace that is
the perfect promise of you.

As your arms hold me safe I realize
my love for you is strong,
my belief in you is limitless,
my admiration for you is constant.

All my wishes have been granted,
and I cherish these quiet blessings you have
given me on this side of heaven.

—*Lori Eberhardy*

Soul Mate

A soul can search a lifetime
with eyes that do not see.
I have found my half in you—
our love was meant to be.

Take my hand and walk with me,
our destiny awaits.
Our love will be our precious guide,
we'll journey to our fate.

Embraced within your tender arms,
I feel that I am free.
I have found my home with you,
Your home is found in me.

—*Betsy Rae Mimnaugh*

Sky Over Sea

Like sky over sea,
so is your love for me.
Our worlds met and wed,
continuing firmaments
of currents and clouds,
stars and sea.
As one woven nature,
we now bless our spirit
with peace and happiness.
The contour of life
covers us two,
like sky over sea,
you and me.

—*Annie Dougherty*

Made for Love

We thank you for love, Holy Creator,
　　that we are made for love,
　　　that learning how to love is our highest destiny,
　　that our race is webbed together
　　　　by bonds of love and caring.

Amen.

—*William Cleary*

A Promise of Love

As we begin our journey,
I can see my reflection in your eyes.
Every time you smile
I know my heart beats because of you.
I will give you the best life has to offer,
and you will always know my love.

You will never have to worry about the rain
or be scared of the dark.
I will give you kisses of faith and hugs of grace,
and in my arms you will be safe.

I promise to support your dreams,
nurture your talents, and encourage your spirit.
You are everything that is genuine and true,
and the world is more beautiful because of you.

As we search to make our place in this world,
I know that anything is possible.
As we aim for the stars, we can expect miracles,
and all good things will be ours.

—*Lori Eberhardy*

Husband and Wife

In the quiet of night
May our words whispered
be tender and consoling;
May our conversations
run deep, touching the soul;
May our laughter
be spontaneous and carefree;
May the ideas we share
shine bright, full of promise;
May our hopes and dreams
be noble, inspired, and united;
May our caresses
be gentle and soothing;
May each embrace
be warm, ardent, and satisfying;
May the prayers we offer
fill our home with peace;
And may our enduring love
for each other glorify Thee.

—*Jennifer Anne F. Messing*

Higher Purpose

May you lean on your beloved's strength
and God's promises
when the day-to-day realities
of work, bills, and stress
sometimes cloud your vision
of what your life together should be.
Know that your purpose
is not to completely understand
all events as they happen,
but rather to replace fear and doubt
with faith and love—
always trusting God for the best
for both of you.

—*Darrell Lindsey*

New Vision

Sharing seasons
          together
   is like seeing everything
           for the first time.

Through your love
          I am born again
   and my whole being
       is alive
     in a new way.

—*Molly Srode*

The Wings of Faith

I close my eyes, spread my wings,
and fall into your love.
I see the peace my heart
is searching for in your eyes.
I hear the warmth in your voice.
A touch of faith becomes a promise of love,
and each day is your gift to me.
I learn there is power in more than one,
so I lay my burdens at your feet.
Your love enhances my life and I feel free.
I will wrap myself around you and
promise you forever.

—Lori Eberhardy

From This Day Forward

From this day forward,
you shall not walk alone.
My heart will be your shelter,
and my arms will be your home.

—*Author unknown*

AUTHOR INDEX

June Cotner is a bestselling author, anthologist, consultant, and speaker. Her books include *Graces, Bedside Prayers, Animal Blessings, Teen Sunshine Reflections,* and *Amazing Graces* (all published by HarperCollins); *Mothers and Daughters, Baby Blessings,* and *Wedding Blessings* (all by imprints of Random House); *Christmas Blessings* (Time Warner); *Forever in Love, Family Celebrations,* and *Comfort Prayers* (Andrews McMeel); *Looking for God in All the Right Places* and *Wishing You Well* (Loyola Press); *Bless the Day* (Kodansha); *Bless the Beasts* (SeaStar Books); *House Blessings* (Cotner Ink); *The Home Design Handbook* (Henry Holt); *Pocket Prayers* (Chronicle Books); and most recently *Miracles of Motherhood* (Center Street/ Hachette Book Group USA).

Altogether, June's books have sold more than 750,000 copies and earned praise in many national publications, including *USA Today, Better Homes and Gardens, Woman's Day,* and *Family Circle.* She has one forthcoming anthology: *Star Light, Star Bright* (Chronicle Books).

June is a graduate of the University of California at Berkeley and the mother of two grown children. She lives in Poulsbo, Washington (a small town outside Seattle), with her husband, two dogs, and one cat. Her hobbies include clogging, yoga, hiking, cross-country skiing, and volunteering at her local elementary school.

June has led workshops for writers and given presentations at bookstores nationwide and at the Pacific Northwest Writer's Association Conference; the Pacific Northwest Booksellers Association Conference; and the Learning Annex schools in New York, San Francisco, Los Angeles, and San Diego. For information on scheduling June as a speaker or workshop leader, you may contact her at one of the addresses listed below.

June Cotner
P.O. Box 2765
Poulsbo, WA 98370
june@junecotner.com
www.junecotner.com

PERMISSIONS AND

ACKNOWLEDGMENTS

Grateful acknowledgment is made to the authors and publishers for the use of the following material. Every effort has been made to contact original sources. If notified, the publishers will be pleased to rectify an omission in future editions.

American Bible Society for scripture taken from the *Good News Translation* (GNT), Second Edition, Copyright © 1992 by American Bible Society. Used by permission.

Martha K. Baker for "A Toast to the Newlyweds" and "The Safe Harbor."

Mike W. Blottenberger for "The Excitable Gift."

Leah Browning for "The Religion of Everyday Things."

Rosalie Calabrese for "On Marriage."

Sally Clark for "A Newlywed's Toast" and "A Newlywed's Prayer."

William Cleary for "Made for Love," "Expanding Hearts," "When Love Is Painful," and "Windy Afternoon."

Kathy Conde for "River."

Barbara Crooker for "When the Acacia Blooms."

Phyllis Joy Davison for "Together Forever."

Marylisa W. DeDomenicis for "Journey."

Division of Christian Education of the National Council of the Churches of Christ in the United States of America for scripture taken from the New Revised Standard Version Bible (NRSV), copyright © 1989, Division of Christian Education of

the National Council of the Churches of Christ in the United
States of America. Used by permission. All rights reserved.

Annie Dougherty for "Sky Over Sea."

Peg Duthie for "More Than One Plus One."

Lori Eberhardy for "The Love Within," "Beloved," "A Promise of
Love," "Devoted," "The Wings of Faith," and "Between You and
Me."

Susan J. Erickson for "Toast to You and Me."

Ida Fasel for "Hands" and "Our Hands."

Maureen Tolman Flannery for "Midnight Wandering" and
"Bedground."

Susan Fridkin for "Yellow Linens."

Charles Ghigna for "So Many Things," "Dreaming Awake," and
"Your Song."

Michael S. Glaser for "Love," "Like God, Perhaps," and "A Blessing
for the Newly Married."

Ingrid Goff-Maidoff for "The Wonder of Your Being," "Divine
Wisdom, Eternal Love," "Keep Your Dwelling Strong," and "Do
Good Things for Each Other."

Marjorie Gray for "Ever Growing" and "Prayer for Fruit."

Penny Harter for "Husband Song," from her book *Lovepoems,*
published by Old Plate Press, copyright © 1981 Penny Harter.
Used by permission of the author.

C. David Hay for "Starshine."

International Bible Society for scripture taken from the Holy
Bible, NEW INTERNATIONAL VERSION® (NIV).
Copyright © 1973, 1978, 1984 International Bible Society. All
rights reserved throughout the world. Used by permission of
International Bible Society.

AJ Kallies for "The Greatest Day."

Joanne Keaton for "Recording Joy."

Candy Killion for "Shine Always."

Shirley Kobar for "Hand in Hand," "Generosity of Spirit," and "Our Bond."

Susan Landon for "Carefree."

Arlene Gay Levine for "Immutable Star" and "Lessons."

Judith A. Lindberg for "Love Comes First" and "Tender Toast."

Darrell Lindsey for "Higher Purpose," "Keep the Joy," "For Those Times Spent Apart," and "Marriage as Prayer."

Eve Lomoro for "Our Lives."

Andrea L. Mack for "A Promise."

Sandra E. McBride for "Sunrise."

David B. McCoy for "Attraction," "Easter Sunday," and "Few Words."

Jennifer Anne F. Messing for "Husband and Wife."

Michelle Close Mills for "Thank You."

Betsy Rae Mimnaugh for "Soul Mate."

Barbara J. Mitchell for "This Morning."

NavPress Publishing Group for scripture taken from The Message. Copyright © 1993, 1994, 1995, 1996, 2000, 2001, 2002. Used by permission of NavPress Publishing Group.

Joan Noëldechen for "The Terms of Love."

Susan R. Norton for "You Complete Me," "Listening," "When the Future Has Come and Gone," and "Lazy Morning Love."

Beatrice O'Brien for "Our Marriage."

Julia Older for "Combinations."

Mary Lenore Quigley for "Moments to Remember."

Zoraida Rivera Morales for "You Are Mine, I Am Yours," "On the Road," "A Toast to Our Family and Friends," "Prayer After a Quarrel," and "Loving."

Linda Goodman Robiner for "Pillow Talk."

Marjorie Rommel for "I Wanted to Tell You."

Rough Stones Music for "Blessing," by Jim Croegaert. Copyright 2005, Rough Stones Music (RoughStonesMusic.com), 827

Sara Sanderson for "So Much for Chores."

Marion Schoeberlein for "Commitment," "The Dark Side of Love," and "When Death Will Come to Part Us."

Monica E. Smith for "Homecoming" and "Mask."

Johanna D. Spangenberg for "Living Realistically."

Molly Srode for "Changing Directions" and "New Vision."

Lois Greene Stone for "Married . . ."

Robin Svedi for "Kismet."

Katherine Swarts for "Ingredients of a Happy Marriage" and "Lasting Love."

Donna Wahlert for "Honeymoon."

Davi Walders for "The Blessing of Yes" and "Seven Wedding Blessings."

Jodi M. Webb for "The Light at the End of the Street."

Erica Staab Westmoreland for "The Language of Love."

Norma Woodbridge for "A Mystery."

Donna Wyland for "Why Do I Love You?"

Michael Young for "The Journey's Start" and "A Blessing Fair."